Second Edition

Activity Book 2

with Online Resources

British English

Caroline Nixon & Michael Tomlinson

Cambridge University Press
www.cambridge.org/elt

Cambridge Assessment English
www.cambridgeenglish.org

Information on this title: www.cambridge.org/9781316628751

© Cambridge University Press 2008, 2014, 2017

First published 2008
Second edition 2014
Updated second edition 2017

40 39 38 37 36 35 34 33 32 31 30 29 28 27 26 25 24

Printed in the Netherlands by Wilco BV

A catalogue record for this publication is available from the British Library

ISBN 978-1-316-62875-1 Activity Book with Online Resources 2
ISBN 978-1-316-62767-9 Pupil's Book 2
ISBN 978-1-316-62786-0 Teacher's Book 2
ISBN 978-1-316-62944-4 Teacher's Resource Book with Online Audio 2
ISBN 978-1-316-62897-3 Class Audio CDs 2 (4 CDs)
ISBN 978-1-316-62861-4 Flashcards 2
ISBN 978-1-316-62853-9 Language Portfolio 2
ISBN 978-1-316-62976-5 Interactive DVD with Teacher's Booklet 2 (PAL/NTSC)
ISBN 978-1-316-62800-3 Presentation Plus 2
ISBN 978-1-316-62868-3 Posters 2
ISBN 978-1-316-62782-2 Monty's Alphabet Book

Additional resources for this publication at www.cambridge.org/kidsbox

Kid's Box

Activity Book 2

Caroline Nixon & Michael Tomlinson

1 Hello again!

1 ✏️ Write.

 I'm Stella.

 I'm Simon.

 I'm Suzy.

She's ___Stella.___ He's _____ _____

 I'm Mr Star.

 I'm Mrs Star.

 I'm Grandpa.

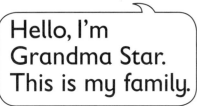 Hello, I'm Grandma Star. This is my family.

_____ _____ _____

2 ✏️ Draw and write.

What's your name? **Me!**

_____

How old are you?

_____

4

3 ✏️ Colour the stars.

1 ⭐⭐☆☆☆☆☆☆☆☆
Colour two stars.

2 ☆☆☆☆☆☆☆☆☆
Colour five stars.

3 ☆☆☆☆☆☆☆☆☆
Colour six stars.

4 ☆☆☆☆☆☆☆☆☆
Colour one star.

5 ☆☆☆☆☆☆☆☆☆
Colour eight stars.

4 ✏️ Match and join.

1	four + one =		7	eight
2	two + one =		5	seven
3	six + one =		8	five
4	eight + one =		6	ten
5	five + one =		9	six
6	seven + one =		10	three
7	nine + one =		3	nine

5 Listen and colour.

6 Listen and point. Write the words.

laelSt   Szuy   onmSi   frou   igteh   sneev

1 This is __Stella.__
She's __eight.__

2 This is _____
He's _____

3 This is _____
She's _____

7 Read the question. Listen and write a name or a number. There are two examples.

Example

What is the boy's name?   _____ *Dan* _____

How old is he?   _____ *9* _____

Questions

(1) What is the girl's name?   _____

(2) How old is the girl?   _____

(3) What is the name of Dan's street?   _____
                                             Street

(4) What number is Dan's house?   _____

(5) What is the name of Grace's book?   _____
                                             House

1 black

2 g_m_

3 s_y

4 b_g

5 c_t

6 pl_y

7 h_nd

8 sn_k_

9 gr_y

10 _pple

9 Listen and write. Match.

a

b

c

d

e

f

g

h

1 _pen_ [b]

2 _____ [ ]

3 _____ [ ]

4 _____ [ ]

5 _____ [ ]

6 _____ [ ]

7 _____ [ ]

8 _____ [ ]

My picture dictionary

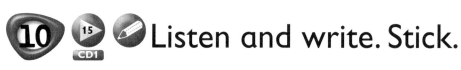 **10** **15** CD1 Listen and write. Stick.

1 _purple_

2 _____

3 _____

4 _____

5 _____

6 _____

My progress

Tick (✓) or cross (✗).

I can count to ten. ☐

I can say the colours. ☐

I can say the alphabet. ☐

1 Find and write the words.

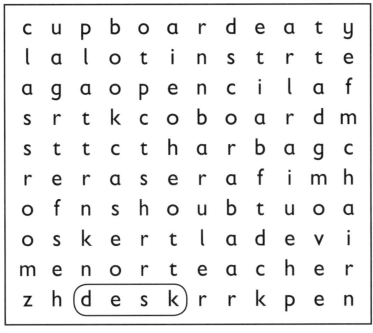

```
c u p b o a r d e a t y
l a l o t i n s t r t e
a g a o p e n c i l a f
s r t k c o b o a r d m
s t t c t h a r b a g c
r e r a s e r a f i m h
o f n s h o u b t u o a
o s k e r t l a d e v i
m e n o r t e a c h e r
z h (d e s k) r r k p e n
```

desk

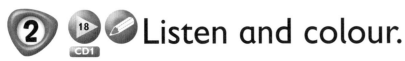

2 **18** CD1 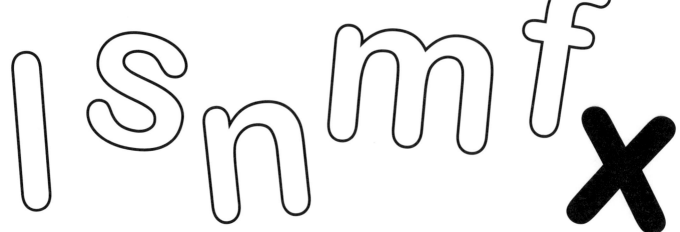 Listen and colour.

l S n m f x

10

3 Look at the numbers. Write the words.

veleen
11

eleven

niffeet
15

- - - - - - - - - -

hiegeetn
18

- - - - - - - - - -

ewletv
12

- - - - - - - - - -

wytent
20

- - - - - - - - - -

reihtnet
13

- - - - - - - - - -

4 Read and colour.

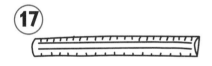

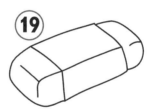

Colour number twelve brown.
Colour number nineteen pink.
Colour number fourteen green.
Colour number seventeen blue.
Colour number sixteen orange.

5 ✏️ **Write the sentences.**

① (a ruler) (There's) (the table.) (on)

There's a ruler on the table.

② (the desk.) (There are) (on) (12 pencils)

_____

③ (There's) (under) (the chair.) (a bag)

_____

④ (the bookcase.) (16 books) (in) (There are)

_____

6 🔍✏️ **Look at the picture. Write the answers.**

① How many burgers are there? *There are six.* _____

② How many apples are there? _____

③ How many oranges are there? _____

④ How many cakes are there? _____

⑤ How many ice creams are there? _____

⑥ How many bananas are there? _____

7 Look and read. Write 'yes' or 'no'.

Examples

There are two teachers in the classroom. _no_

There's a poster on the wall. _yes_

Questions

(1) There is a door next to the cupboard. _ _ _ _ _ _

(2) There is a board on the wall. _ _ _ _ _ _

(3) There are two tables under the board. _ _ _ _ _ _

(4) There is a ruler on a bookcase. _ _ _ _ _ _

(5) There are three cars under the desk. _ _ _ _ _ _

 **8** **25** **CD1** ✏ **Listen and colour red or green.**

① red

② green

③ tree

④ ten

⑤ pen

⑥ read

⑦ twelve

⑧ fourteen

⑨ teacher

⑩ desk

9 🔍 ✏ **Find the words.**

buschoolegreyellowhiteraseruleredesk

How many colours are there? _____

What are they? _____

14

My picture dictionary

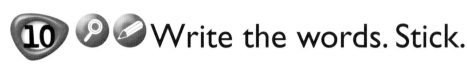 **10** Write the words. Stick.

taechre	baodr	rlure
teacher	- - - -	- - - -
skde	bkoocsae	cpubaord
- - - -	- - - -	- - - -

My progress

Tick (✓) or cross (✗).

I can talk about my classroom. ☐

I can say the numbers 11–20. ☐

I can spell. ☐

Marie's maths Block graphs

💬✏️ **Ask and answer. Colour the graph.**

Which animals do you like?

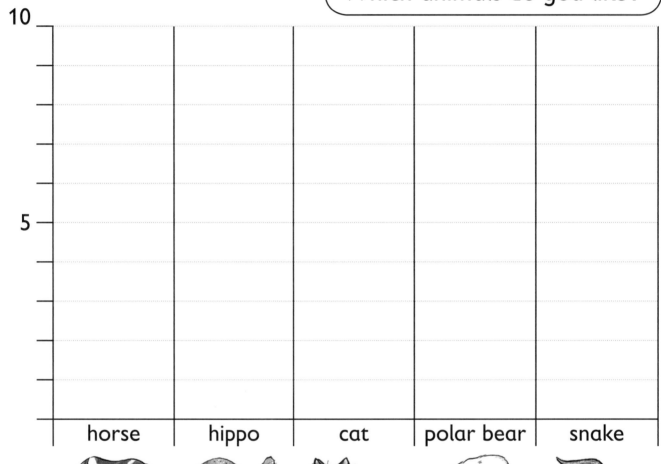

horse	hippo	cat	polar bear	snake

2 🔍✏️ **Answer the questions.**

1 How many children like horses? _ _ _ _ _ _ _ _ _ _

2 How many children like hippos? _ _ _ _ _ _ _ _ _ _

3 How many children like cats? _ _ _ _ _ _ _ _ _ _

4 How many children like polar bears? _ _ _ _ _ _ _ _ _ _

5 How many children like snakes? _ _ _ _ _ _ _ _ _ _

3 Read and complete.

| come in   Yes, of course.   After you.   Can you spell |

①

- Can we _____come in_____, please?
- Yes, come in.

②

- _____
- Thank you.

③

- _____
  ruler, please?
- Yes, r-u-l-e-r.

④

- Can you open the window, please?
- _____

4 Draw a picture of you. Be polite!

Me!

3 Play time!

1 🔍✏️ Read. Circle the toy words. Write.

k i t e

_____ _____

_____

Suzy's got a ⟨kite⟩. Simon's got a robot. Lenny's got a train. Meera's got a car. Stella's got a computer game. Alex has got a big yellow watch.

____ _____

2 🔊33 CD1 ✏️ Listen and tick (✔) the box.

3 ✏️ Complete the sentences and colour the pictures.

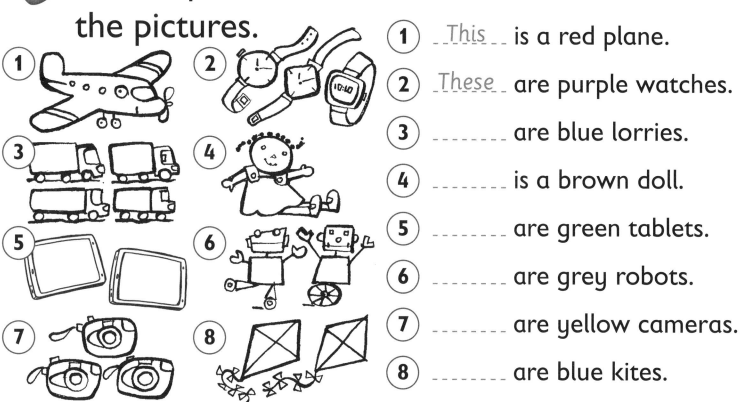

1. _This_ is a red plane.
2. _These_ are purple watches.
3. _____ are blue lorries.
4. _____ is a brown doll.
5. _____ are green tablets.
6. _____ are grey robots.
7. _____ are yellow cameras.
8. _____ are blue kites.

4 ✏️ Match. Write the words.

k	_kitchen_ _kite_	~~itchen~~ ~~ite~~
c	_____ _____	amera ake
r	_____ _____	uler obot
d	_____ _____	oll og
tr	_____ _____	ousers ain
pl	_____ _____	ease ane

Listen and colour. Then answer.

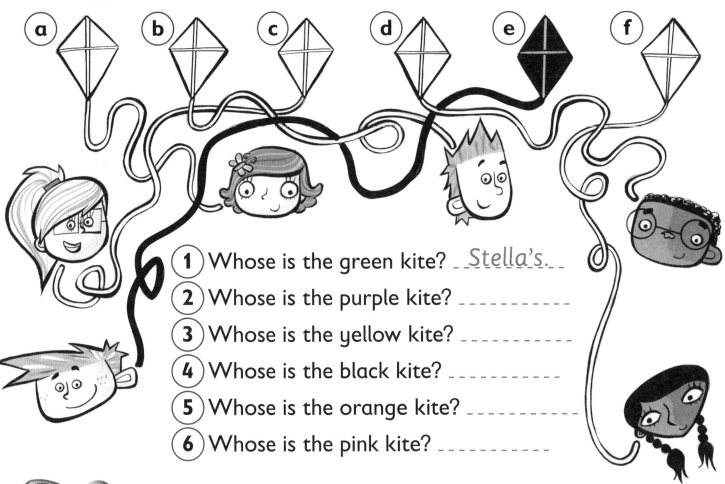

a b c d e f

1 Whose is the green kite? _Stella's._

2 Whose is the purple kite? _____

3 Whose is the yellow kite? _____

4 Whose is the black kite? _____

5 Whose is the orange kite? _____

6 Whose is the pink kite? _____

6 **Write the questions.**

1 _Whose is the lorry?_ _____ It's Bill's.

2 _____ It's Lucy's.

3 _____ It's Ben's.

4 _____ It's Kim's.

5 _____ It's Tony's.

7 🔍✏️ Look and read. Put a tick (✔) or a cross (✗) in the box. There is one example.

Examples

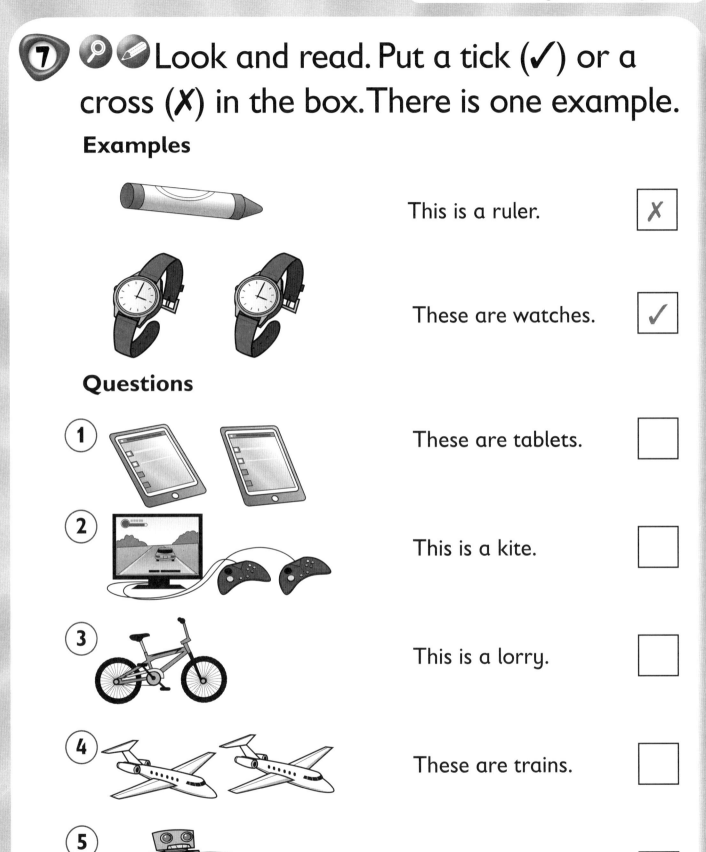

This is a ruler.	✗
These are watches.	✔

Questions

1	These are tablets.	
2	This is a kite.	
3	This is a lorry.	
4	These are trains.	
5	This is a robot.	

8 CD1 42 ✏ Listen and write the words.

① ~~fish~~   ② ~~kite~~   ③ pink   ④ five   ⑤ my

⑥ swim   ⑦ bike   ⑧ big   ⑨ fly   ⑩ sit

fish

kite

9 CD1 43 ✏ Listen and join the dots.

14

6 •

3

5

2

17 •

19

1

8   11   13   10

20

What is it?   It's a _____ .

My picture dictionary

  Listen and stick. Write the words.

① ___kite___	② _ _ _ _ _ _	③ _ _ _ _ _ _
④ _ _ _ _ _ _	⑤ _ _ _ _ _ _	⑥ _ _ _ _ _ _

My progress

Tick (✓) or cross (✗).

I can talk about my favourite toy. ☐

I can write 'toy' words. ☐

23

4 At home

1   Listen and draw lines.

Bill   Dan   Alice   Eva

Matt   Pat   Lucy

2 Write the words.

m	¹a	t		

| | | ³ | | |

| | | ⁶ | | |

| | | | | |

| | ⁷ | ² | | ⁸ |

| ⁴ | | | | |

| | ⁵ | | | |

| | | | | |

1	2	3	4	5	6	7	8

3 Read and write the number. Draw.

sixteen = __16__ → m	twelve = _____ → s
fourteen = _____ → l	fifteen = _____ → a
seventeen = _____ → r	thirteen = _____ → i
eighteen = _____ → o	nineteen = _____ → f
twenty = _____ → p	

(1)

m					
16	13	17	17	18	17

Me!

(2)

14	15	16	20

(3)

12	18	19	15

4 Read and write the words.

mirror ~~bedroom~~ mat face bath

My bathroom is next to my (1) _bedroom_. In my bathroom,
I sit in the (2) _____ and wash my body. On the wall, there
is a (3) _____ . You can see your (4) _____ in it.
There is a blue (5) _____ on the floor. You can stand on it.

5 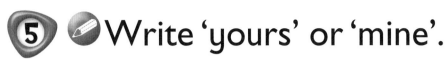 Write 'yours' or 'mine'.

1. Whose is this?
   It's _mine_.

2. Is this _____ or Simon's?
   It's mine.

3. Is this _____ ?
   Yes, it is.

4. Whose are these?
   They're _____.

6 53 CD1 Listen and colour.

7 Listen and draw lines. There is one example.

Mark   Sue   Kim   Grace

Nick   Hugo   Matt

27

8 🎵58 CD1 ✏️ Listen and write the words.

(1) ~~boat~~ (2) ~~box~~ (3) doll (4) phone (5) clock

(6) clothes (7) yell<u>ow</u> (8) <u>l</u>orry (9) socks (10) sofa

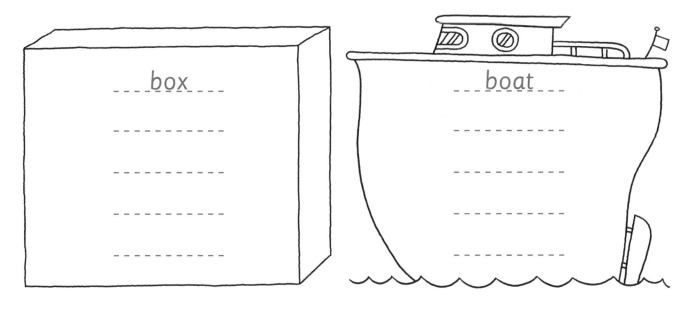

box

boat

9 ✏️ Write the words.

This   ~~That~~   These   Those   These   That

(1) ___That___ is a sofa.

(2) _____ is a phone.

(3) _____ are armchairs.

(4) _____ is a clock.

(5) _____ are mats.

(6) _____ are beds.

28

10  Complete the words. Stick.

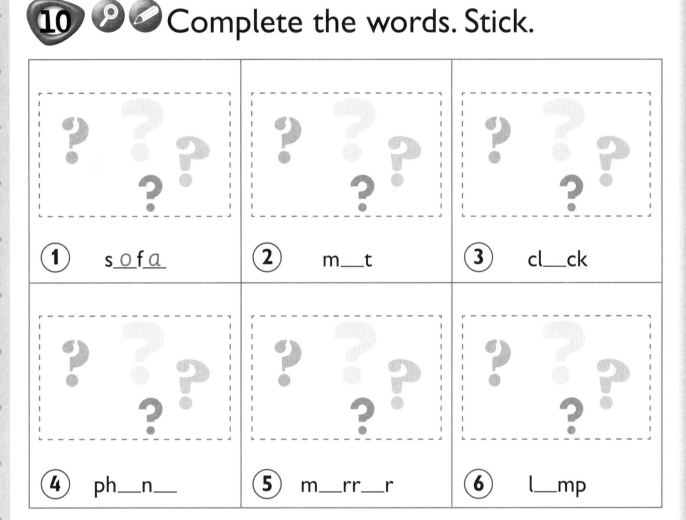

1 s _o_ f _a_

2 m __ t

3 cl __ ck

4 ph __ n __

5 m __ rr __ r

6 l __ mp

My progress

Tick (✓) or cross (✗).

I can talk about my house. ☐

I can say what's mine. ☐

Marie's art Origami

1 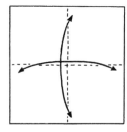 Make a jumping frog.

 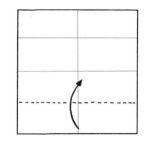 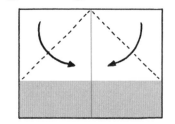 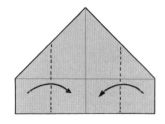

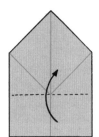 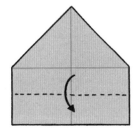 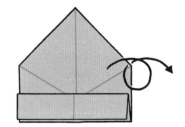 

2 Look and write.

~~robot~~ sofa cupboard kite phone lamp

①

robot

②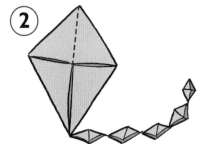

_____

③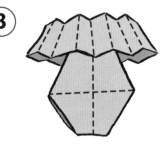

_____

④

_____

⑤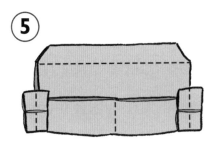

_____

⑥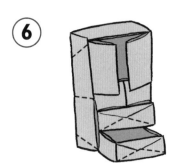

_____

3  Look, read and match.

① 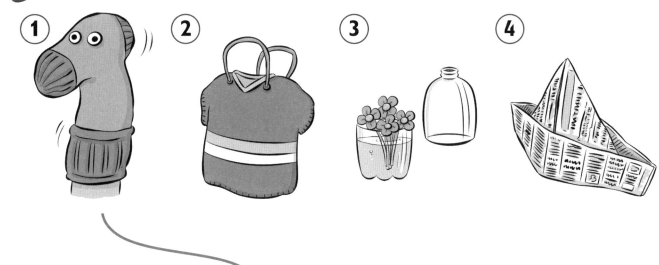 ② ③ ④

ⓐ an old
T-shirt

ⓑ an old
sock

ⓒ old paper

ⓓ a plastic
bottle

4 You've got four boxes, two socks, a
T-shirt and five pencils. Draw a robot.

Review

1 ✏️ Match the colour.

7 grey	nine	8 yellow	three	5 pink
6 blue	ten	two	10 orange	four
five	3 purple	9 green	eight	1 brown
2 red	seven	six	4 black	one

2 🔊 5 CD2 ✏️ Listen and write the number.

3 ✏️ Write the questions. Answer the questions.

	a	b	c	d	e	f
1	what	lorries	dirty	how	big	bed
2	shoes	toy	clean	small	balls	whose
3	is	small	camera	many	are	chair
4	there	under	where	on	the	or

1 4c 3e 4e 1b

Where are the lorries _____ ?

_____ .

2 2f 2b 3a 4d 4e 1f

_____ ?

_____ .

3 3e 4e 2a 2c 4f 1c

_____ ?

_____ .

4 1d 3d 1b 3e 4a

_____ ?

_____ .

5 4c 3a 4e 3c

_____ ?

_____ .

6 1a 3a 4d 4e 3f

_____ ?

_____ .

1 🔍✏️ **Read and write the names.**

This is Lenny and his family. He's with his brother Sam, his sister May, and his cousin Frank. Lenny's brother has got a big nose. Lenny has got small eyes. Lenny's cousin is young. He's a baby. Lenny's sister has got long hair.

2 ✏️ **Write the words.**

~~sofa~~ ~~mum~~ ~~plane~~ ~~bookcase~~ teacher grandma baby
kite desk lorry grandpa playground cousin bath robot
board mirror boat lamp dad bed ruler doll phone

In the house
sofa

Family
mum

Toys
plane

At school
bookcase

3 Read. Write the name. Colour.

Hello. This is my family. My mummy's got long purple hair, small green ears and five yellow teeth. Her name's Trudy. My daddy's name's Tom. He's got short red hair and a dirty green nose. He's got eight brown teeth. My brother Tony's got long brown hair, big red eyes and one white tooth. My sister's name is Tricia. She's very clean! She's got big ears, short blue hair, orange eyes and six green teeth.

4 Write the words.

bbya   afntharedrg   anthmoredrg   oremth

sstire   fthrea   dda   csinou   rthbore   mmu

baby

baby

5 🔊 ✏️ **Listen and write the number.**

6 🔍 ✏️ **Look at the pictures and write the letters.**

1 - What are you doing, Mum?

   - I'm making a cake. `c`

`d`

2 - Whose kite are you flying, Simon?

   - I'm flying your kite, Suzy.

3 - What are you eating, Dad?

   - I'm eating chocolate ice cream.

4 - Whose shoes are you cleaning, Grandpa?

   - I'm cleaning Simon's shoes.

5 - Which word are you spelling, Stella?

   - I'm spelling 'beautiful'.

6 - What are you drawing, Grandma?

   - I'm drawing Stella.

7 📀 13 CD2 ✏️ Listen and tick (✔) the box.
There is one example.

Example

What is Dan doing?

Questions

① Which girl is Anna?

② What's Sue doing?

③ What's Grandpa doing?

④ What's Sam drawing?

8 🔊15 ✏️ **Listen and write.**

1. bu̲s
2. sh___
3. m_m
4. S___
5. s_n
6. r_ler
7. bl___
8. r_n
9. j_mp

9 ✏️ **Write the letters.**

a	He's kicking	his car.	[ ]
b	They're cleaning	in her bed.	[ ]
c	He's driving	a football.	a
d	She's sleeping	books.	[ ]
e	We're singing	a song.	[ ]
f	I'm playing	the guitar.	[ ]
g	They're reading	their teeth.	[ ]

My picture dictionary

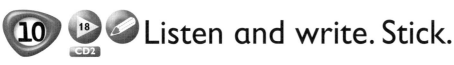 Listen and write. Stick.

1 _grandma_

2 _____

3 _____

4 _____

5 _____

6 _____

My progress

Tick (✓) or cross (✗).

I can talk about my family. ☐

I can talk about actions. ☐

6 Dinner time

1 🔍✏️ Read the lists and find the food.

Draw lines with a pencil.

Draw lines with a pen.

a) Shopping list
- oranges
- bread
- rice
- bananas
- apples
- milk
- ice cream
- burgers
- apple juice
- eggs
- water

b) Shopping list
- potatoes
- rice
- bread
- carrots
- fish
- orange juice
- chips
- chicken
- lemons
- meat

Start

Start

Finish

Finish

2  Find and colour.

Colour the pears green.
Colour the carrots orange.
Colour the tomatoes red.

Colour the chicken brown.
Colour the meat red.
Colour the lemons yellow.

3 Draw and write about your favourite food. Ask and answer.

Me!

What's your favourite food for dinner?

It's chicken and chips.

My favourite food is _ _ _ _ _ _ _ _

_ _ _ _ _ _ _ _ _ _ _ _ _ _ _ _ _ _

_ _ _ _ _ _ _ _ _ _ _ _ _ _ _ _ _ _

_ _ _ _ _ _ _ _ _ _ _ _ _ _ _ _ _ _

4 🔊 25 CD2 ✏️ Listen and tick (✓) or cross (✗).

① ✗
② ☐
③ ☐
④ ☐

5 🔍 ✏️ Read and write the numbers.

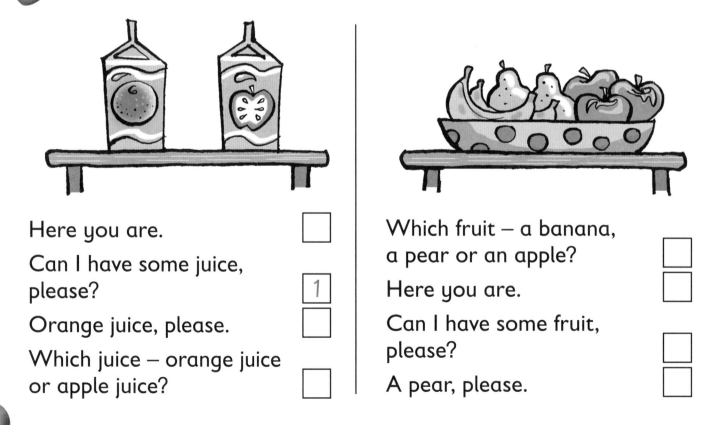

Here you are. ☐

Can I have some juice, please? 1

Orange juice, please. ☐

Which juice – orange juice or apple juice? ☐

Which fruit – a banana, a pear or an apple? ☐

Here you are. ☐

Can I have some fruit, please? ☐

A pear, please. ☐

6 🔍✏️ Read and choose a word from the box. Write the word next to numbers 1–5. There is one example.

My breakfast

I eat my breakfast in the ___kitchen___ . I sit on a (1) _____ at

the table. My dad and my (2) _____ sit with me. My favourite

drink for breakfast is (3) _____ and I eat an (4) _____

with lots of bread. I don't like fruit. My dad loves fruit and he has

two (5) _____ every morning for his breakfast.

Example

~~kitchen~~   egg   bananas   lunch

mirrors   chair   milk   brother

7   Listen and write the words.

| teacher | chair | watch | ~~children~~ | chicken | kitchen | lunch | chips |

1 _children_

2 _____

3 _____

4 _____

5 _____

6 _____

7 _____

8 _____

8 Write the words and the letters.

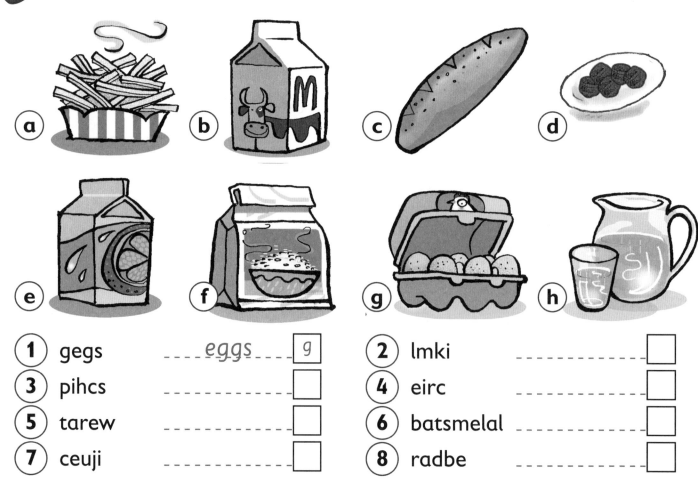

a   b   c   d

e   f   g   h

1 gegs _____eggs_____ [g]   **2** lmki _____ [ ]

3 pihcs _____ [ ]   **4** eirc _____ [ ]

5 tarew _____ [ ]   **6** batsmelal _____ [ ]

7 ceuji _____ [ ]   **8** radbe _____ [ ]

My picture dictionary

9 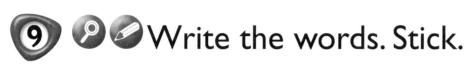 Write the words. Stick.

ckinehc	gegs	pchis
chicken		
lkmi	rcie	dearb

My progress

Tick (✓) or cross (✗).

I can talk about my favourite food. ☐

I can talk about breakfast, lunch ☐
and dinner.

I can ask and answer questions ☐
about food.

45

1 **Read and match.**

| milk | meatballs | eggs | lemons | potatoes | carrots |

Now you! 2 **Write the words.**

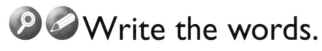

apples potatoes milk carrots eggs lemons
meat chicken bananas rice pears tomatoes

From animals …   From plants …   From trees …

3 Draw your favourite food.

milk   bread   eggs   juice   chicken   rice   water   fish
carrots   apples   meatballs   potatoes   bananas   oranges

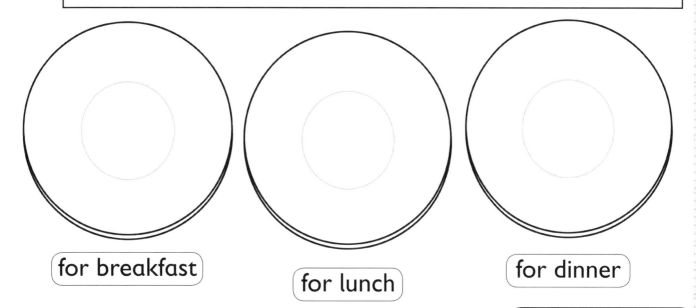

for breakfast

for lunch

for dinner

4 Now tell your partner.
Draw your friend's food.

What's your favourite food for breakfast?

I like oranges and apples.

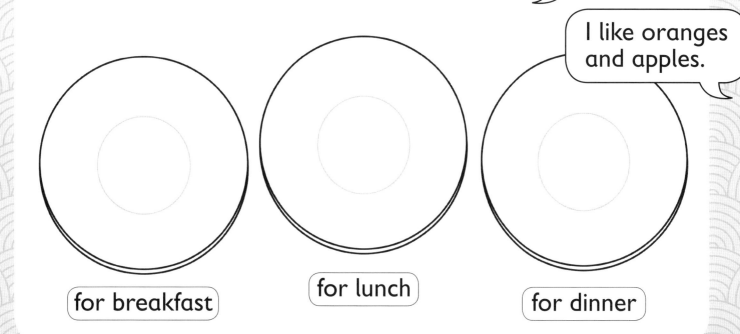

for breakfast

for lunch

for dinner

1 🔍✏️ Find and write the words.

w	a	l	e	r	s	d	s	p	i
s	h	e	e	p	t	u	p	l	d
e	d	m	e	y	k	c	i	r	a
p	m	i	u	s	a	k	d	b	y
t	h	c	h	i	c	k	e	n	a
e	w	t	o	g	o	y	r	o	b
c	a	s	r	z	w	i	l	s	i
h	f	i	s	h	e	t	r	h	r
a	r	t	e	l	i	z	a	r	d
m	o	u	s	e	f	r	e	n	d
s	g	o	a	t	r	f	r	e	v

horse

2 🔍✏️ Read. Draw and write the words.

~~snakes~~ ~~crocodiles~~ fish   lizards   birds   giraffes   tigers   monkeys

This is the Star Zoo. The birds are next to the snakes. The fish are under the birds. The lizards are between the fish and the monkeys. The yellow and brown animals next to the monkeys are giraffes. The big orange and black cats under the crocodiles are tigers.

snakes

crocodiles

3 ✏️ Draw lines.

💬✏️ Now ask your friend and draw lines.

> Where is the donkey?

> It's in the cupboard.

4 🔊 38 CD2 ✏️ **Write the words. Listen and check.**

| love | I | So | do | I | love | lizards | don't |

1

a I _love_ spiders.

b So do _____ .

2

c _____ love fish.

d _____ do I.

3

e I love _____ .

f So _____ I.

4

g I _____ goats.

h I _____ .

5 ✏️💬 **Draw your favourite animal. Ask your friend.**

What's your favourite animal?

Me!

I love _____ .

6 Listen and colour. There is one example.

7 **42** **CD2** **Listen and write.**

①
<u>sp</u>ider

②
__ar

③
__ake

④
__im

⑤
__irt

⑥
__ow

⑦
__ella

⑧
____ool

8 **Write the 'animal' words.**

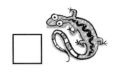

Down

① This is small and black and it's got eight legs.

② We get eggs from this farm bird.

⑥ This farm animal can eat clothes.

Across

① This farm animal has got white hair.

② We get milk from this big farm animal.

③ This green or brown animal has got four short legs, a long body and a long thin tail.

④ This bird has got orange feet. It can swim.

⑤ This small green animal has got big feet and long legs. It can swim and jump.

⑦ This big animal has got big ears.

9   Listen and stick. Write the words.

① _spider_

② _____

③ _____

④ _____

⑤ _____

⑥ _____

My progress

Tick (✔) or cross (✗).

I can write 'animal' words. ☐

I can talk about things I love. ☐

8 My town

1 🔍✏️ Look and read. Tick (✓) or cross (✗) the box.

 (1) This is a flat. ✗

 (2) These are boots. ☐

 (3) This is a hospital. ☐

 (4) This is a street. ☐

 (5) This is a park. ☐

 (6) This is a café. ☐

2 ✏️ Circle the different word.

(1) car	lorry	bus	(boot)
(2) flat	town	goat	street
(3) bike	café	hospital	school
(4) kitchen	bedroom	bathroom	park
(5) shop	cupboard	armchair	sofa
(6) street	park	school	bedroom
(7) frog	hospital	café	flat
(8) door	town	window	floor

3 Spot the differences.

PET SHOP
Rosa's Café
BUS
A

TOYS
BOOKS
B

1. In A *there's one car*, but in B *there are two cars*.
2. In A ______________, but in B ______________.
3. In A ______________, but in B ______________.
4. In A ______________, but in B ______________.
5. In A ______________, but in B ______________.
6. In A ______________, but in B ______________.

4 Write the words.

~~skateboard~~ ~~pear~~ ~~chair~~ ~~dog~~ coconut armchair table bike apple computer game lizard pineapple cat train car lemon lorry fish mouse mirror clock orange bird cupboard

FRED'S FRUIT
pear
TED'S TOYS
skateboard
Pete's Pets
dog
Phil's Furniture
chair

5 **Listen and colour the stars.**

1 2 3

4 5 6

7 8 9

 6 **Read and write the names.**

Tom

You're Tom. You're sitting in front of Jill.
You're Ann. You're sitting between Tom and Nick.
You're Bill. You're sitting behind Nick.
You're Sue. You're sitting between Jill and Bill.

7 Look at the pictures and read the questions. Write one-word answers.

Examples

Where are the people?   at a ____café____

How many children are there?   ____two____

Questions

1 Where is the dog?   under the _____

2 What has the boy got?   an _____

3 What is the dog doing?   _____

4 Who is sad?   the _____

5 What is the dog doing now? _____
the ice cream

8   Listen and write the words.

| cow | mouse | ~~brown~~ | house | mouth | down | trousers | town |

1 **2** **3** **4**

brown

5 **6** **7** **8**

sit

9 Draw a town. Use these words.

| pet shop | café | bookshop | hospital | flat | park |

Me!

My picture dictionary

10 🔍✏️ Complete the words. Stick.

① fl_a_t	② p__rk	③ sh__p
④ h__sp__t__l	⑤ str____t	⑥ c__f__

My progress

Tick (✔) or cross (✗).

I can talk about the town. ☐

I can write about the town. ☐

1 Listen and say the animal.

cat   bird   frog   elephant   sheep   cow

It's a bird.   They're cats.

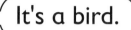

Now you! 2  Make a guitar.

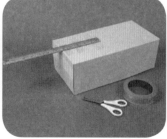

3 🔍✏️ Read and circle.

① There's a **red** / **green** man on the traffic lights. You can cross the road.

② Don't ride your skateboard **on the road** / **at the park**.

③ The sign says: **Don't walk** / **Walk** on the grass.

④ Put your **rubbish** / **books** in the bin.

⑤ Don't cross the road. The traffic lights are **green** / **red**.

4 🔍✏️ Look and write 'can' or 'can't'.

① I __can__ put my rubbish here.

② I _____ walk here.

③ I _____ cross the road here.

④ I _____ play here.

Review

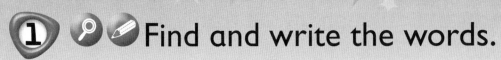

1 🔍✏️ **Find and write the words.**

'food' words

milk

_____

_____

_____

_____

t	g	d	r	t	y	z	x	d	j	u
b	r	e	a	k	f	a	s	t	u	w
r	a	a	m	u	m	g	y	c	i	g
o	n	w	n	m	c	j	x	h	c	h
t	d	a	d	d	t	o	s	i	e	e
h	m	s	l	o	i	i	p	k	d	
e	o	p	a	b	h	k	s	s	i	
r	t	m	i	l	k	t	s	m	n	
o	h	c	k	s	o	i	e	m	g	n
o	e	g	g	s	j	u	r	x	k	e
g	r	a	n	d	f	a	t	h	e	r

'family' words

brother

_____

_____

_____

_____

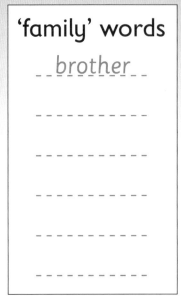

2 ▶️6 CD3 ✏️ **Listen and write the number.**

1

3   Read and draw lines.

The baby is behind the door.
The mother is between the bed and the desk.
The clock is on the bookcase, between the books.
The lamp is on the desk.
The polar bear is on the desk, in front of the lamp.
There's a spider under the bed.

4   Listen and complete. Chant.

Whose Which ~~Who~~ What How many Where who How old What

1 ___Who___ is that?
That's my brother, Paul.

2 _____'s he doing?
He's catching a ball.

3 _____ ball is it?
It's my cousin Nick's.

4 _____ is he?
He's very young.
He's only six.

5 _____ is he now?
He's in the hall.

6 _____'s he doing?
He's throwing his ball.

7 _____ balls have you got?
I don't know!
We've got a lot.

8 _____ one's your favourite – red or blue?
I don't know!

9 And _____ are you?

9 Our clothes

1 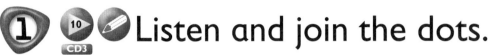 Listen and join the dots.

2 Follow the 'clothes' words.

watch	shoes	glasses	lizard	cake
thing	frog	socks	burger	sheep
hat	T-shirt	jeans	carrots	goat
trousers	ice cream	cow	bread	spider
dress	skirt	jacket	shirt	handbag

How many 'clothes' words are there? _____

Write the 'animal' words. _____

Write the 'food' words. _____

9

3 ✏️ Write the words and colour the picture.

a	b	c	d	e	f	g	h	i	j	k	l	m
☆	■	○	▬	◆	◧	●	★	◈	△	▼	⌣	◑

n	o	p	q	r	s	t	u	v	w	x	y	z
◢	★	◤	◇	▲	⌣	▽	□	▬	◗	▽	▭	◸

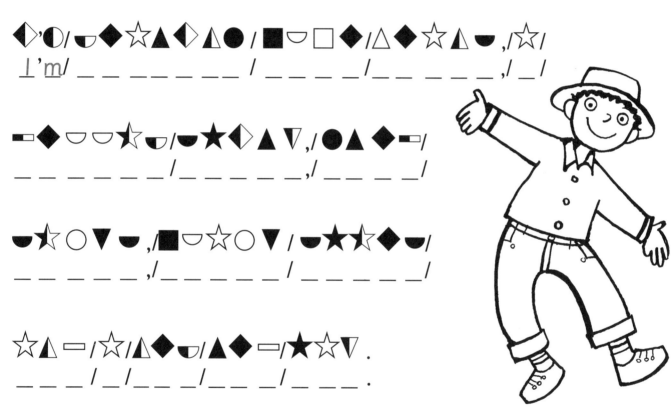

I'm/ _ _ _ _ _ _ _ / _ _ _ _ _/_ _ _ _ _ _,/ _ _/

_ _ _ _ _ _ _ _ _/ _ _ _ _ _,/ _ _ _ _/

_ _ _ _ _,/_ _ _ _ _/ _ _ _ _ _/

_ _ _ _/ _ _/ _ _ _ _/ _ _ _/ _ _ _ .

4 ✏️ Describe your clothes.

Me!

I'm wearing _____

_____

_____

_____

5 🔍 ✏️ Look and write.

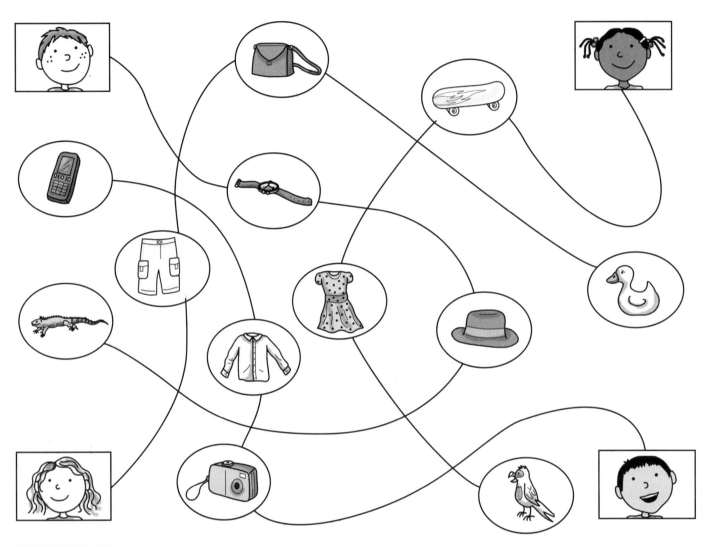

 I've got <u>a watch, a hat and a lizard.</u>

 I've got

 I've got

 I've got

6 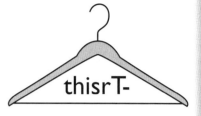 Look at the pictures. Look at the letters. Write the words.

Example

T-s h i r t

thisrT-

Questions

1  _ _ _ _ _

rsesd

2  _ _ _ _ _

snjae

3 _ _ _ _ _ _

srtsho

4 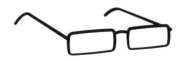 _ _ _ _ _ _ _

ssslega

5  _ _ _ _ _ _ _

bghdaan

7 🔊18 CD3 ✏️ Listen and write *s* or *sh*.

1. s h eep
2. __oe
3. _even
4. chip_
5. __irt
6. de_k
7. fi__
8. dre__
9. _leep
10. __op

8 🔍💬 Cross out five objects. Ask your friend.

Have you got a boot?

Yes, I have.

hat	☐	lemon	☐
handbag	☐	cow	☐
boot	✓	sheep	☐
glasses	☐	monster	☐
frog	☐	tomato	☐

My picture dictionary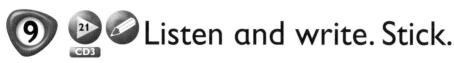

9 **21** **CD3** ✏️ Listen and write. Stick.

① _handbag_	**②** ____	**③** ____
④ ____	**⑤** ____	**⑥** ____

My progress

Tick (✓) or cross (✗).

I can talk about my clothes. ☐

I can talk about things I have got. ☐

10 Our hobbies

1 ✏️ Write the words and the numbers.

① ② ③ ④ ⑤ ⑥

ptingain ___painting___ [4]   itagur _____ ☐

btonadmin _____ ☐   tleab nisten _____ ☐

hokeyc _____ ☐   ebbasall _____ ☐

2 🔵24 CD3 ✏️ Listen and colour.

③ ✏ Write the words.

Down ↓   Across →

④ ✏ Complete the sentences.

① ↓ They're _____playing_____ _____table tennis_____

④ → They're _____

⑤ ↓ She's _____

⑥ → They're _____ _____

⑦ → She's _____

⑨ → He's _____

5 🎧 27 CD3 ✏️ Listen and tick (✓) or cross (✗).

1 a ☑ b ☐ c ☐

2 a ☐ b ☐ c ☐

3 a ☐ b ☐ c ☐

4 a ☐ b ☐ c ☐

6 ✏️ Draw and write about you.

My name's ----------------------------------- .

I'm ------------------------------- years old.

My hair is ------------------------------- .

My eyes are ------------------------------- .

My favourite toy is ------------------------- .

I like ------------------------------------- .

I don't like ------------------------------- .

I love ------------------------------------- .

My favourite hobby is --------------------- .

Me!

Look and read. Write 'yes' or 'no'.

Example

Two boys are playing hockey.   yes

A girl is playing tennis.   no

Questions

(1) A boy is wearing a black T-shirt.   ---------

(2) Two boys are playing table tennis.   ---------

(3) A tall girl is playing basketball.   ---------

(4) The boy under the tree is playing the guitar.   ---------

(5) A girl in a white skirt is playing badminton.   ---------

8  Listen and match.

CD3

1. A lo**ng** dog. _c_
2. The boy's eati**ng.** _____
3. She's si**ng**i**ng** a so**ng.** _____
4. The ki**ng**'s readi**ng.** _____
5. She's painti**ng.** _____

a

b

c

d

e

9 Read. Write the words.

Hello. I'm Tom. Now, I'm at
_____school_____ . I'm playing
_____ . I'm wearing
a red and white _____
and long blue _____ .
I like doing sport.
For lunch today, I've got
some _____ and an
_____ . I like having
lunch at school.

My picture dictionary

10 Write the words. Stick.

bdanimtno	tbale tneins	bsaeblal
badminton		
bakstebllla	pniatngi	oeyckh

My progress

Tick (✔) or cross (✘).

I can write 'sport' and 'hobby' words. ☐

I can talk about my likes. ☐

Now you! **1**  Find, draw and write.

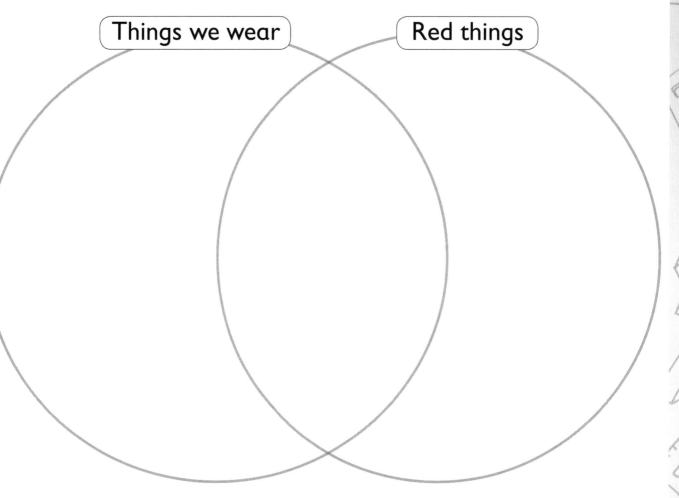

Things we wear

Red things

2 Write about your Venn diagram.

There are _____ red things.

There are _____ things we wear.

There are _____ red things we wear.

3 🔍✏️ **Look and tick (✓) or cross (✗).**

1

You can run with the ball.
Right rule? ☐
Wrong rule? ☐

2

You can throw the ball.
Right rule? ☐
Wrong rule? ☐

3

You can kick the ball.
Right rule? ☐
Wrong rule? ☐

4

You can hit the ball with a
tennis racket.
Right rule? ☐
Wrong rule? ☐

4 **Listen and say the sport.**

It's basketball.

11 My birthday

1 ✏️ Write the letters and the words.

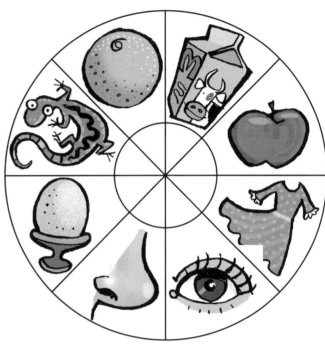

_ _ _ u _ _ _ _ _ _   _ _ _ _ _ _ _ _ _

2 🔍 ✏️ Circle the different words.

1 tree	garden	flower	(car)
2 shoe	camera	robot	kite
3 sausage	armchair	chicken	fries
4 lemonade	orange	milk	water
5 badminton	basketball	soccer	bus
6 café	desk	hospital	school
7 cupboard	bed	sofa	kitchen
8 kitchen	hall	bathroom	mirror

3 **Listen and draw.**

4 **Write the words.**

| me | you | her | it | us | ~~them~~ |

1

Look at ___them___ .

2

Can I play with _____ ?

3

Smile at _____ .

4

Take a photo of _____ .

5

Come and play with _____ .

6

Take a photo of _____ .

5 ✏️ Write the sentences.

1 (fries?) (some) (Would) (like) (you)

Would you like some fries?

2 (some) (please.) (cake,) (like) (I'd)

----

3 (Would) (like) (you) (to play) (us?) (with)

----

4 (to play) (I'd) (table tennis.) (like)

----

6 🔍✏️ Read and write the information.

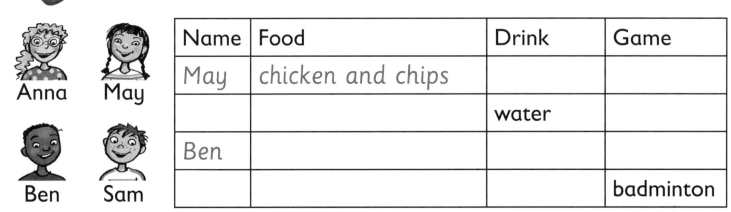

Name	Food	Drink	Game
May	chicken and chips		
		water	
Ben			
			badminton

It's Anna's birthday and she's having lunch with her three friends, May, Ben and Sam.

1 May would like some chicken and chips and she'd like some orange juice.

2 Ben would like some meatballs and potatoes.

3 One boy would like some sausages and tomatoes, and he'd like some water.

4 Two children would like some lemonade.

5 The two boys would like to play hockey and the two girls would like to play badminton.

6 One girl would like some carrots and rice. It's her birthday today.

7 Listen and draw lines. There is one example.

Tom Jill Dan May

Mark Hugo Kim

8 **Listen and write the words.**

| skirt | bird | ~~purple~~ | thirteen | burger | shirt | girl | birthday |

① ....purple........ **②** .... **③** .... **④** ....

⑤ .... **⑥** .... **⑦** .... **⑧** ....

9 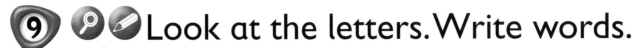 **Look at the letters. Write words.**

Happy birthday, Simon.
It's your garden party.

........young........ ....

....

....

....

....

....

  Listen and stick. Write the words.

① ___cake___

② ___ ___ ___

③ ___ ___ ___

④ ___ ___ ___

⑤ ___ ___ ___

⑥ ___ ___ ___

My progress

Tick (✓) or cross (✗).

I can ask for food and drink. ☐

I can talk about party food. ☐

12 On holiday!

1 **CD4** Listen and tick (✓). Find the words.

1. sea ✓ she
2. song sun
3. sand hand
4. shell she
5. mountain mouth
6. three tree
7. floors flowers
8. bird big
9. animals apples
10. phone fish
11. holiday today

a	s	m	o	b	s	a	n	r
f	h	o	l	i	d	a	y	h
l	e	u	t	r	e	n	g	m
o	l	n	i	d	f	i	s	h
w	l	t	s	u	n	m	e	t
e	m	a	g	s	e	a	f	r
r	u	i	h	k	h	l	o	e
s	a	n	d	a	r	s	t	e

2 Match. Write the words.

h	hockey	holiday		ockey	oliday
b				eautiful	each
m				ountain	ouse
s				and	un
sh				ell	irt
tr				ain	ees

84

3  Look at the picture and answer the questions.

1. How many people are there? ...... *There are four people.* ......
2. What's the man drinking? _____
3. What's the woman doing? _____
4. Is the dog walking? _____
5. Where's the boy swimming? _____
6. What's the girl picking up? _____
7. How many birds are there? _____
8. Where's the jellyfish? _____

4 Look at the letters and write the words.

1. dnas

   ...... *sand* ......

2. leshl

   _____

3. leyljhifs

   _____

4. chaeb

   _____

5. erte

   _____

6. nanitomu

   _____

5 **8 CD4** **Listen and tick (✓) the box.**

1. What does Nick want to do?
   a □
   b ✓
   c □

2. What does Mary want to have for lunch?
   a □
   b □
   c □

3. What does Peter want for his birthday?
   a □
   b □
   c □

4. What does Susan want to drink?
   a □
   b □
   c □

5. What does Sally want to play?
   a □
   b □
   c □

6. Where does John want to go?
   a □
   b □
   c □

6 **Read. Write 'Yes, he does' or 'No, he doesn't'.**

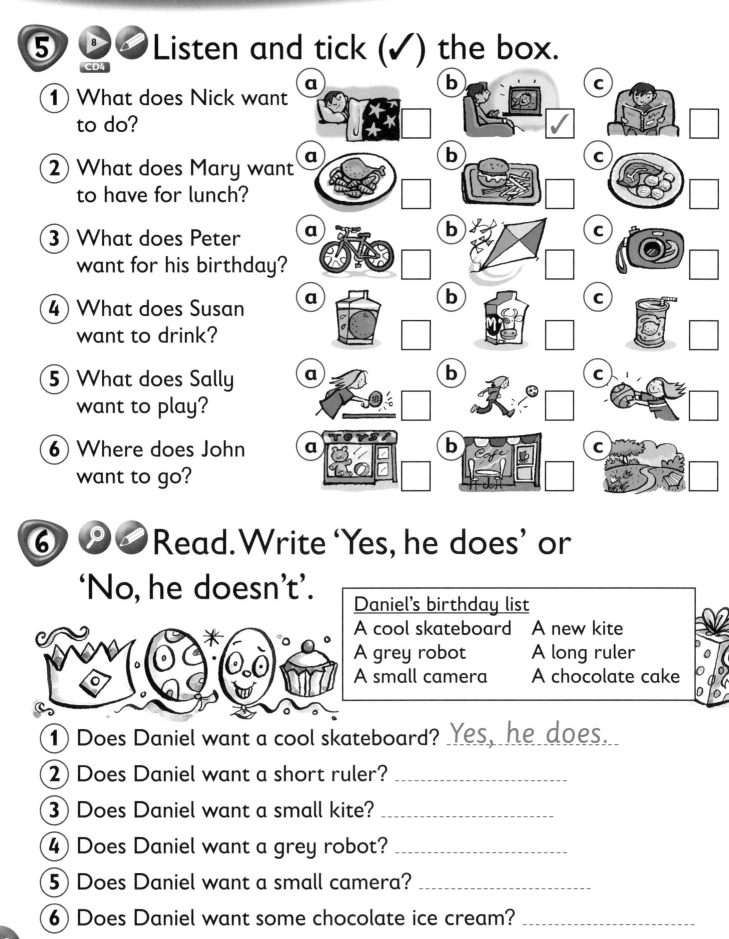

Daniel's birthday list	
A cool skateboard	A new kite
A grey robot	A long ruler
A small camera	A chocolate cake

1. Does Daniel want a cool skateboard? _Yes, he does._

2. Does Daniel want a short ruler? _____

3. Does Daniel want a small kite? _____

4. Does Daniel want a grey robot? _____

5. Does Daniel want a small camera? _____

6. Does Daniel want some chocolate ice cream? _____

7 Listen and colour. There is one example.

8 🔺13 CD4 ✏️ Listen and match.

1. Dad catches his ...   fish.
2. Ben gets ...   dog.
3. Jill swims with the ...   hat.
4. Tom stops the ...   sun.
5. Mum runs in the ...   shells.

(a) _2_   (b) ___   (c) ___   (d) ___   (e) ___

9 ✏️ Complete the questions. Then answer.

ugly   new   short   ~~small~~   dirty

1. Is your kitchen big or _____ *small* _____ ?

   _____

2. Is your city beautiful or _____ ?

   _____

3. Is your street long or _____ ?

   _____

4. Is your bedroom clean or _____ ?

   _____

5. Is your school old or _____ ?

   _____

My picture dictionary

10 🔍✏️ Complete the words. Stick.

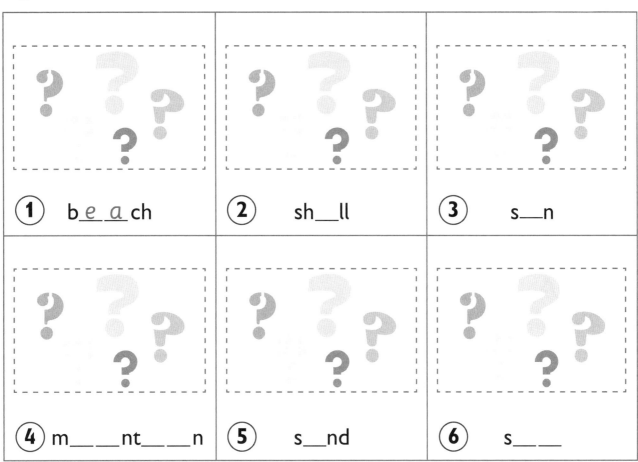

① b_e_ _a_ ch

② sh__ll

③ s__n

④ m_____nt_____n

⑤ s__nd

⑥ s_____

My progress

Tick (✓) or cross (✗).

I can talk about my holidays. ☐

I can talk about what I want. ☐

Read, draw and colour.

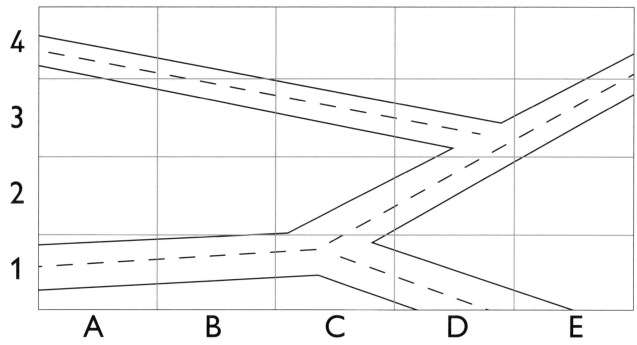

Draw a car in one square. Colour it blue.

Draw a tree in one square. Colour it brown and green.

Draw a flower in one square. Colour it purple and green.

Draw a house in one square. Colour it red.

Draw a mountain in one square. Colour it grey.

2 **Ask and answer. Draw.**

Where is the car?

D5.

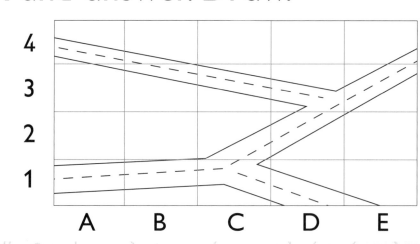

3   Listen and write the number.

1

4 Write and draw.

Me!

Review

1 🔊 20 CD4 ✏️ Listen and join the dots.

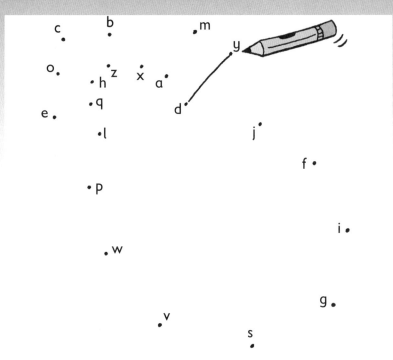

What's this? It's a _____ .

2 🔊 21 CD4 ✏️ Listen and colour. There is one example.

3 🔍✏️ Match the questions and answers.

(1) Whose shorts are they? [f]   (a) He's cooking.

(2) Where are they playing badminton? [ ]   (b) On the beach.

(3) Who's that? [ ]   (c) The long, red one.

(4) What colour's your shirt? [ ]   (d) It's green.

(5) What's Mr Star doing? [ ]   (e) She's my cousin.

(6) Which dress is yours? [ ]   (f) They're mine.

4 🔍✏️ Read and complete.

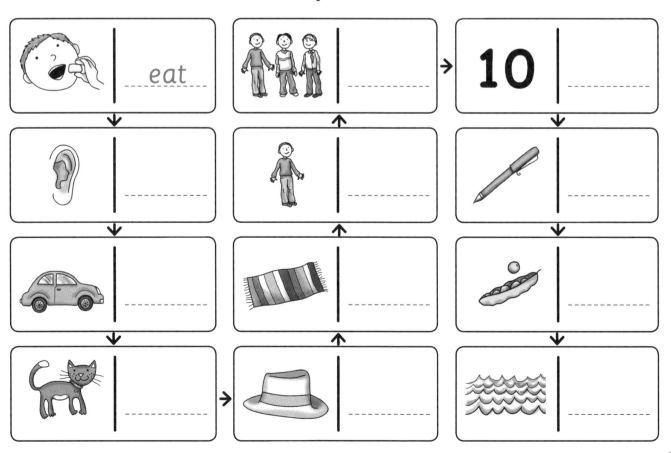

eat

10

Grammar reference

1 Order the words.

1 (Tom.) (What's) (his) (He's) (name?)

_____ ? _____

2 (Who's) (She's) (Mrs) (Brown.) (my) (teacher,) (she?)

_____ ? _____

2 Look and write.

| Yes, there is.   Yes, there are.   No, there aren't. |

1 Is there a whiteboard on the wall? ✓ _____

2 Are there three computers in the classroom? ✗ _____

3 Are there a lot of chairs in the classroom? ✓ _____

3 Circle the question and the answer.

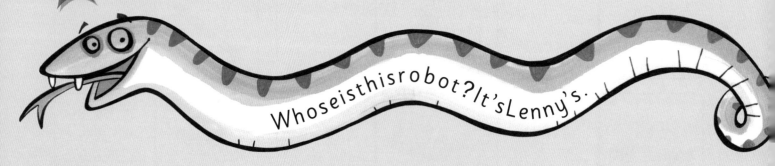

Whoseisthisrobot?It'sLenny's.

4 Match the questions and answers.

1 Whose is that red dress?   Yes, they are.

2 Whose blue trousers are those?   It's mine.

3 Are those blue boots yours?   They're Dad's.

5 Look and complete.

'm not	'm	're	're not	's	's not

1. ✓ I _____ singing.
2. ✗ I _____ dancing.
3. ✓ You _____ reading.
4. ✗ He _____ running.
5. ✓ She _____ playing tennis.
6. ✗ We _____ painting.

6 Circle the question and the answer.

Canlhavesomefish,please?Hereyouare.

7 Look and write.

So do I.	I don't.	So do I.

1. I like rabbits. ☺ _____
2. I like donkeys. ☺ _____
3. I like spiders. ☹ _____

8 Look and complete.

1. Where's the café? It's **bhnide** _____ the school.
2. Where's the park? It's **ni ofrnt fo** _____ the hospital.
3. Where's the shop? It's **teewenb** _____ the park and the flats.

9 Write the answers.

| haven't. has. hasn't. have. |

1. Have you got a skateboard?   ✓ Yes, I _ _ _ _ _ _ _ _ _
2. Has he got red shorts?   ✗ No, he _ _ _ _ _ _ _ _ _
3. Has she got a blue bag?   ✓ Yes, she _ _ _ _ _ _ _ _
4. Have you got grey boots?   ✗ No, I _ _ _ _ _ _ _ _

10 Look and complete.

| love   don't like   likes   doesn't like |

1. ♥ ♥ I _ _ _ _ _ _ _ _ _ _ _ _ _ _ _ _ reading.
2. ♥ He _ _ _ _ _ _ _ _ _ _ _ _ _ _ _ playing badminton.
3. ✖ She _ _ _ _ _ _ _ _ _ _ _ _ _ singing.
4. ✖ I _ _ _ _ _ _ _ _ _ _ _ _ _ cooking.

11 Look and complete.

| No, thank you.   Yes, please. |

1. Would you like some meatballs?   ✓ _ _ _ _ _ _ _ _ _ _ _ _ _ _ _ _ _ _ _
2. Would you like some milk?   ✗ _ _ _ _ _ _ _ _ _ _ _ _ _ _ _ _ _ _ _

12 Look and complete.

| I want to   I don't want to |

1. ☺ _ _ _ _ _ _ _ _ _ _ _ _ _ _ _ go to the beach.
2. ☹ _ _ _ _ _ _ _ _ _ _ _ _ _ go to a big city.

Hello again! (page 9)

 **black**  purple 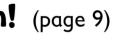 yellow

green pink blue

 Back to school (page 15)

MAT
$2 \times 1 = 2$
$2 \times 2 = 4$
$2 \times 3 = 6$
$2 \times 4 = 8$
$2 \times 5 = ?$

 Play time! (page 23)

Can
you
Spell?

At home (page 29)

 # Meet my family (page 39)

 # Dinner time (page 45)

At the farm (page 53)

 My town (page 59)

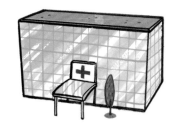

 Our clothes (page 69)

Our hobbies (page 75)

 # My birthday (page 83)

 # On holiday! (page 89)